KILKENNY CASTLE

Dúchas The Heritage Service

An **Roinn Ealaíon, Oidhreachta, Gaeltachta** ⁊ **Oileán**
DEPARTMENT of ARTS, HERITAGE, GAELTACHT and the ISLANDS

Text
Paddy Friel

Design
Peggy McConnell

Photography
Con Brogan
Gerry Deegan

Illustrations
Jenny Baker

Typesetting
Boethius

Dúchas The Heritage Service
Dept. of Arts, Heritage, Gaeltacht and the Islands

ISBN 0-946617-08-2

Abbreviations
NLI National Library of Ireland
NGI National Gallery of Ireland

Poem *Kilcash*
by permission of Dolmen Press

All illustrations, unless otherwise stated,
from Kilkenny Castle.

Dublin: Published by Stationery Office.
To be purchased from any bookseller or directly
from the
GOVERNMENT PUBLICATIONS SALE OFFICE,
Sun Alliance House, Molesworth Street, Dublin 2.

The Butler coat of arms over the Main Gate. The motto "comme je trouve" means "as I find" CB

Kilkenny Castle has been standing for over eight hundred years, dominating Kilkenny city and the south-east of Ireland. It was originally built as the symbol and reality of Norman control in the area, and it has continued throughout the many different periods of Irish history to symbolise the fortunes of one of the most powerful Irish families, the Butlers of Ormonde.

The Butler family, Earls, Marquesses and Dukes of Ormonde, lived here in Kilkenny Castle for five hundred and fifty years. They were a remarkable family, resilient, politically astute, and faithful to the Crown and to Ireland after their fashion. These loyalties determined their fortunes and career, and so too the fortunes of their seat, Kilkenny Castle. When the Butlers prospered, Kilkenny Castle was rebuilt and redecorated; when they fell from grace, the castle became run-down and dilapidated. So the story of Ireland and the Butlers is also the story of Kilkenny Castle.

In state care since 1969, the castle today also represents the story of a society and a way of life that effectively no longer exists, of kings and knights, cavaliers and roundheads, lords and ladies. And of course that of landlord and tenant, of master and servant.

The Castle and grounds are now a National Historic Park in the care of Dúchas The Heritage Service of Dept. of Arts, Heritage, Gaeltacht and the Islands.

KILKENNY CASTLE

THE TOWN OF KILKENNY

There has been a castle on this site since 1172 when the Norman knight, Richard de Clare, called Strongbow, built a wooden tower on this rocky height overlooking the River Nore.

The first stone castle was built here twenty years later by Strongbow's son-in-law, William Marshall, Earl of Pembroke. This was a square-shaped castle with towers at each corner: three of these original four towers survive today.

A busy and successful commercial centre grew around the original Norman settlement, and the present Hightown and Irishtown areas of Kilkenny today date from that period. Indeed, in the middle ages one of the main gateways into the walled town was through the south gate of this castle.

Throughout the following two centuries the Normans intermarried and integrated with the native Irish, becoming "more Irish than the Irish themselves". The Statutes of Kilkenny (1366) was an attempt to stop this absorption and gaelicisation by making intermarriage between the two groups a crime equal to high treason.

But the name Kilkenny (Cill Chainnigh) predates all these events. It comes from a much earlier inhabitant, Saint Canice, who founded a monastery here in the sixth century, about five hundred years before either the Normans or the Butlers. Saint Canice's monastery occupied the site where the beautiful twelfth-century St Canice's Cathedral is today.

Round tower, St Canice's Cathedral GD

12th Century

A MEDIEVAL CASTLE

Tomb of Piers Rua Butler (d. 1539) and his wife Mairgread Ní Gearoid, or Margaret Fitzgerald, daughter of the eighth Earl of Kildare

Piers spent all of his life intriguing to establish his claim to the title — one of his rivals was Thomas Boleyn, ancestor of Anne Boleyn. Piers eventually triumphed in 1538 and was the first of the Earls of Ormonde to be buried in St Canice's Cathedral.

Piers and his wife set up the original Kilkenny College, and also brought Flemish workers to Kilkenny in an attempt to establish a weaving industry here. GD

Tomb of Richard Butler, 1st
Viscount Mountgarret
(d. 1571) in St Canice's
Cathedral GD

St Canice's Well GD

Detail from the fireplace in the Long Gallery. The Butler offers the King his first cup of wine CB

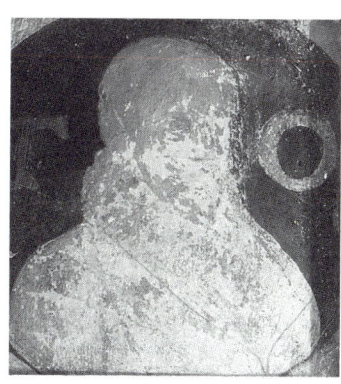

WHO WERE THE BUTLERS?

The Butlers of Kilkenny Castle were an Anglo-Norman family who came to Ireland in 1171 in the first wave of the Norman invasion.

Originally their name was Walter, but they changed the family name to Butler because of a royal privilege that the astute Theobald Walter managed to acquire. In 1185, the king of England made him Chief Butler of Ireland, a title which made him a sort of senior toastmaster at the Coronation Banquet—he would offer the new king his first cup of wine—and which, more importantly, gave him prisage or butlerage (i.e. *a duty or leverage*) on all wines imported into these two islands. To mark this valuable honour—and no doubt to ensure its continuation—the family dropped the name Walter and assumed the name Le Botiller or Butler.

The Walter/Butler wealth and influence increased rapidly. They acquired enormous tracts of land in Tipperary and Kilkenny, and in the last years of the fourteenth century James Butler, by now also third Earl of Ormond, bought Kilkenny Castle and installed himself there as undisputed ruler of the area.

Their Walter origins were now forgotten. The Butler dynasty that was to dominate the south-east of Ireland for over five hundred years was now firmly established.

Now that they had money and power and prestige, the Butlers of the sixteenth and seventeenth centuries lived the lives of minor aristocrats, politically and socially closer to English mores than to the life-styles of the native Irish chieftains. Black Tom, or Tomas Dubh, is a typical example of a young earl of the time.

As a young man he had been sent to the English court to acquire 'civility'. This experience confirmed him in his loyalty to the Crown and indeed impressed him so deeply that, when he returned to Ireland as tenth Earl of Ormond, he built a beautiful manor house at Carrick-on-Suir in County Tipperary and decorated the walls with stucco representations of himself and Queen Elizabeth (who called him ambiguously her *"Black Husband"*).

But there was also a Gaelic element in his life. He had a longstanding feud with the not-so-loyal Earls of Desmond over boundaries in the Clonmel area. This Ormond-Geraldine quarrel was a century old. Finally it came to a pitched battle in 1565 at Affane on the River Suir. Desmond was defeated in what was the last private pitched battle in these islands.

When Black Tom died, his daughter inherited all his lands, while his titles passed to a nephew. After years of disputes and claims, this was resolved in 1629 when the nephew's grandson, James Butler, twelfth Earl of Ormond, married his cousin, Elizabeth Preston. This meant that the Butler titles, wealth and lands were cleverly united and consolidated again.

CONFLICTING LOYALTIES

The middle of the seventeenth century saw the struggle between the king and parliament in England. In Ireland people were also torn. The Butlers, too, were caught up in this struggle.

A Confederate Council was set up. This breakaway alliance of Irish and Old English held their alternative parliament in Kilkenny for seven years (*1642-48*), trying to determine their own affairs in Ireland.

James Butler, twelfth Earl of Ormond, had been raised in England as a ward of court, and had tremendous personal loyalty to both King Charles I and his son, Prince Charles. Ormond was now the king's Lord Lieutenant in Ireland, and Commander of his army, while throughout this time a Butler cousin, Viscount Mountgarret, was prominent in the Confederate Council.

Affairs in England defeated them all. After a civil war, King Charles I was executed, and Oliver Cromwell came to power. Butler went into exile with Prince Charles, while Cromwell proceeded through Ireland ruthlessly restoring his control. In 1650 he attacked Kilkenny, battering the now-missing south wall of the Castle before the town surrendered.

Throughout the years of parliamentary control and Ormond's exile, Lady Ormond held on tightly to the Butler lands and properties. Letters she wrote to Cromwell stated that they were her inheritance and so could not be forfeit for her husband's treason. Her claim succeeded.

Oliver Cromwell NGI

James Butler (1610-1688),
12th Earl, 1st Marquess and
1st Duke of Ormonde "The
Great Duke" CB

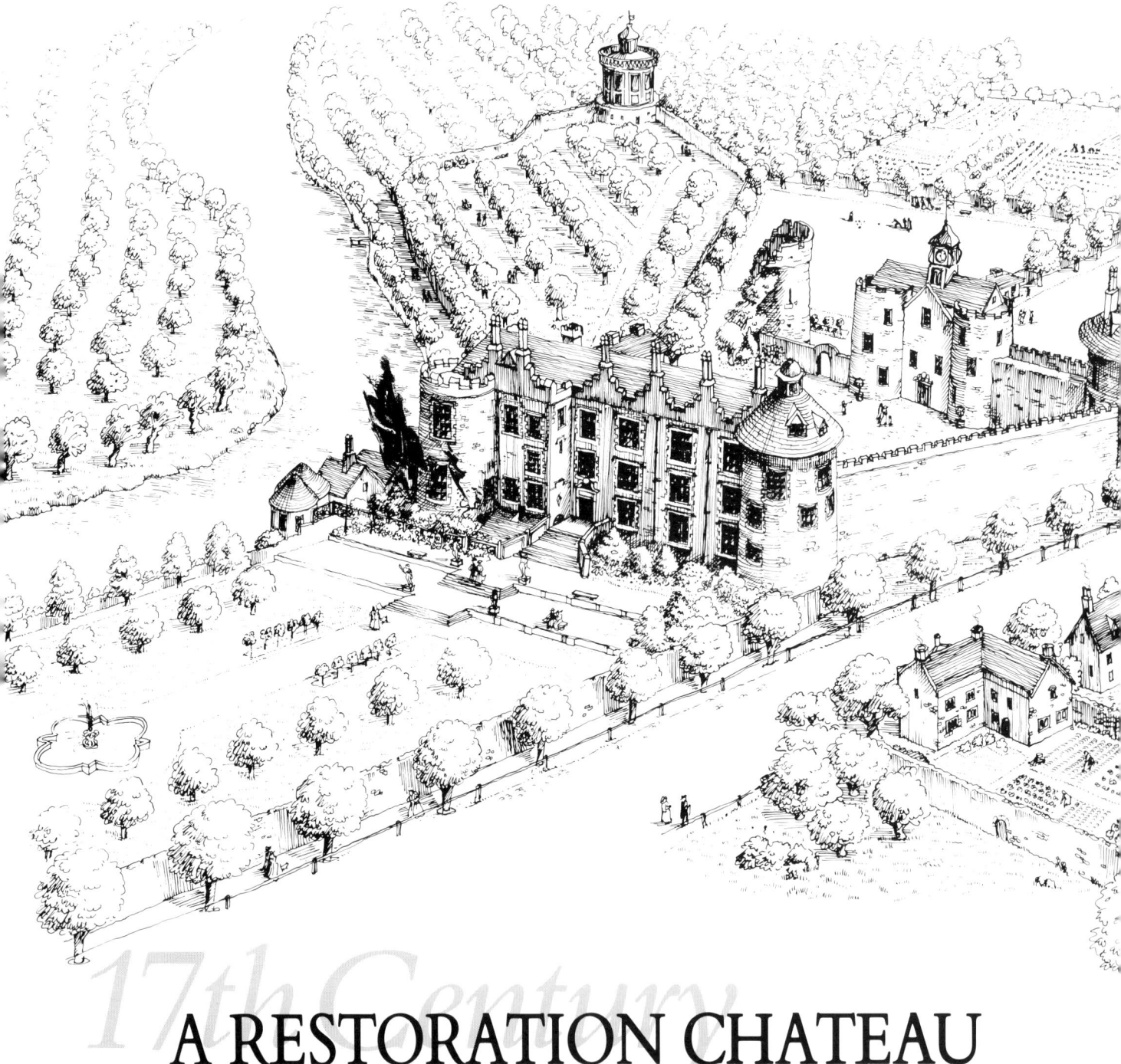

17th Century

A RESTORATION CHATEAU

THE GREAT DUKE

In 1660, King Charles II returned triumphantly to England and James Butler was with him. They had been in exile together for ten years, moving between the courts of Europe. But now all their powers and wealth were to be restored to them. In 1661, Butler was made Duke of Ormonde and Knight of the Garter. A year later he returned with great celebration to Ireland. Based in Dublin Castle, he now began his second term as Lord Lieutenant of Ireland.

He now had the difficult task of re-establishing the king's authority in Ireland. The Cromwellian campaigns and following plantations now meant very many claims and lawsuits over land. Despite the problems of such a task, Ormonde did his best and his reputation as a statesman grew. Naturally he also reinstated the Butler family interests in Ireland too.

The Duke and his Duchess lived as part of the Restoration court. The old feudal Castle in Kilkenny was renovated and became an elegant French chateau which was the marvel of all who visited. The most up-to-date furniture, tapestries and paintings decorated Kilkenny Castle in a style fitting for the Great Duke.

Ormonde was Lord Lieutenant again from 1677 to 1682, when he oversaw a return of prosperity to Ireland. He founded the Royal Hospital at Kilmainham in Dublin for retired soldiers, based on what he had seen at Les Invalides in Paris. This, in turn, inspired the Chelsea Hospital in London. The Great Duke also kept for public use the lands that now form the Phoenix Park in Dublin.

Of himself, James Butler said, *I have all this while served my master faithfully, and according to his own direction, which way I intend to pursue to the end. Yet I have not been neglectful of my country, and the fruits of my care of it may be felt when I am gone, if they will not be their own greatest enemies.*

He died in 1688 and is buried in Westminster Abbey in London.

Fireplace detail: the triumphal return of Ormonde to Dublin

Many great titles and positions were given to the Butlers. The elaborate royal charters of these honours are in Ormonde Castle.

This tapestry is one of a series "The History of Decius" bought by the Great Duke and which still hangs in the Castle CB

LOYALTY AND LOSS

In the last years of the seventeenth century, England—and Ireland—was divided again. King James II had been deposed, and his daughter Mary, with her husband William of Orange, were invited to take the throne. This developed into a war in Ireland as James tried to defeat William and reclaim the throne in a series of pitched battles known as 'Cogadh an dá Rí', or the Williamite wars.

The Butlers were naturally involved in this crucial struggle. The second duke, James Butler, was a very famous and experienced soldier who decided to join William's cause, while a catholic cousin, Lord Galmoy, held Kilkenny Castle and entertained King James here. In 1690 the two kings met at the Battle of the Boyne. James was defeated. Ormonde then recovered his castle and was host to King William soon after.

Ormonde was once more closely involved in affairs at court. On the death of Queen Anne, however, he decided to support the Stuart claim to the throne. As this was treasonable, in 1716 Ormonde fled to exile on the continent. In his absence he was found guilty and his estate forfeit. He died thirty years later in Rome.

The Butler estates and titles in Ireland passed to James' brother, Charles, Earl of Arran. He did not claim these, feeling it politically unwise, and so when he died without an heir in 1758, the titles of Duke and Marquess of Ormonde became extinct. The title of Earl passed to catholic cousins in Kilcash, County Tipperary.

View of Kilkenny Castle and City c. 1695, by Francis Place NGI

THE PENAL TIMES

The eighteenth century in Ireland was the age of the Penal Laws. These were a series of laws designed to ensure protestant control in Ireland by means of a detailed oath of allegiance to the Crown which catholics could not take. This effectively excluded them from parliament, from holding any public office, from entering the law, or from holding a commission in the army or navy. Further laws forbade catholics from buying land, or from renting on other than a short lease. The practice of the catholic religion was also outlawed.

This meant that the old gaelic way of life was now in real decline, with their great houses closing. An Irish poet wrote a great lament, 'Caoineadh Cill Chais' about the Butler castle of Kilcash and its "good lady", Lady Margaret Butler. He describes how the rich traditional society, which supported many poets like himself, is drawing to an end.

Window in Kilcash Church

Kilcash Castle, County Tipperary (above)

Cill Chais

Cad a dhéanfaimid feasta gan adhmad?
Tá deireadh na gcoillte ar lár;
níl trácht ar Chill Chais ná ar a teaghlach
is ní bainfear a cling go bráth.
An áit úd a gcónaíodh an deighbhean
fuair gradam is meidhir thar mhnáibh,
bhíodh iarlaí ag tarraingt tar toinn ann
is an t-aifreann binn á rá.

Ní chluinim fuaim lachan ná gé ann,
ná fiolar ag éamh cois cuain,
ná fiú na mbeacha chun saothair
thabharfadh mil agus céir don tslua.
Níl ceol binn milis na n-éan ann
le hamharc an lae a dhul uainn,
ná an chuaichín i mbarra na ngéag ann,
ós í chuirfeadh an saol chun suain.

Tá ceo ag titim ar chraobha ann
ná glanann le gréin ná lá,
tá smúid ag titim ón spéir ann
is a cuid uisce go léir ag trá.
Níl coll, níl cuileann, níl caor ann,
ach clocha is maolchlocháin,
páirc an chomhair gan chraobh ann
is d'imigh an géim chun fáin.

Kilcash

Now what will we do for timber,
with the last of the woods laid low?
There's no talk of Cill Chais or its household
and its bell will be struck no more.
That dwelling where lived the good lady
most honoured and joyous of women
—earls made their way over wave there
and the sweet Mass once was said.

Ducks' voices nor geese do I hear there,
nor the eagle's cry over the bay,
nor even the bees at their labour
bringing honey and wax to us all.
No birdsong there, sweet and delightful,
as we watch the sun go down,
nor cuckoo on top of the branches
settling the world to rest.

A mist on the boughs is descending
neither daylight nor sun can clear.
A stain from the sky is descending
and the waters receding away.
No hazel nor holly nor berry
but boulders and bare stone heaps,
not a branch in our neighbourly haggard,
and the game all scattered and gone.

RECLAMATION AND RESTORATION

By the second half of the eighteenth century Kilkenny Castle was very badly run-down, just as the fortunes of the Butler family and of Ireland were. But outside pressures — the wars with America and then with France — meant that England needed to be sure of Irish loyalty, and so the Penal Laws had to be relaxed.

Walter Butler of Garryricken, inherited the Butler titles and lands in 1766, and decided to move into the very dilapidated castle. His son, John, had married the heiress Anne Wandesford, of Castlecomer, and Walter and John spent much of his inheritance on the castle. They re-routed the old approach road away from the castle, built a new road, and then landscaped and planted the castle park and the road much as it is today. They built the beautiful stables and courtyards across this road, and finally Walter moved to his newly-built dower house, Butler House, beyond those stables.

After his father's death, in 1783, John Butler reclaimed the title of seventeenth Earl of Ormonde. This was confirmed in 1791.

The Butlers rapidly re-established their position and prestige. They always had large areas of land in Kilkenny and Tipperary, and now were able to become the largest landowners in the south-east.

The next earl, Walter Butler, joined fashionable society in London. He became a companion of the Prince Regent, who subsequently recreated the title of Marquess of Ormonde for him. Partly to sustain his extravagant lifestyle, Walter gave up his hereditary right to the Butler wine tax to the Crown in 1811 for £216,000, a enormous sum of money at that time.

Walter's brother, James, would later succeed him. James Butler represented Kilkenny in the Irish parliament in Dublin for four years up to the Act of Union in 1800. He was against replacing the Irish parliament with Irish seats in the Houses of Commons and Lords, in London, but represented Kilkenny for a further twenty years there.

Walter Butler of Garryricken
(1703-1783) CB

Eleanor Morres, his wife
(1711-1794) CB

19th Century

A VICTORIAN COUNTRY HOUSE

THE VICTORIANS

The nineteenth-century Butlers were typical of their time, very solidly wealthy, with agents who ran their vast estates very effectively and efficiently. They served with a suitable regiment, married well, and enjoyed their well-ordered lives.

In 1826, a major programme of work started to restore Kilkenny Castle to its supposed 'mediaeval' appearance, and also to bring it up to date as a country house with all appropriate modern conveniences. The east wing was completely rebuilt to house the large family picture collection in a new Long Gallery, and the west curtain wall built out to provide more bedrooms.

For the years 1845–50 Ireland suffered disastrously through the Great Famine. For four years blight destroyed the potato crop and people suffered dreadfully. About a million people died, and a similar number emigrated. Landlords' reactions varied, and the Butlers are said to have dealt reasonably with their tenants, reducing or waiving rents in some cases, arranging passages to the colonies in others.

In 1854, further work to Kilkenny Castle started. The earlier *porte cochere* was extended to become the front hall linking the two wings, the Moorish staircase built, and many other details and decorations completed.

At the turn of the century, James Butler, twenty-first Earl and third Marquess of Ormonde, entertained King Edward VII and Queen Alexandra here, and later, King George V and Queen Mary. They enjoyed shooting together over Ormonde's vast estates in Kilkenny and Tipperary, they all sailed together at Cowes, and Lord and Lady Ormonde had their place at all state functions.

Frances Paget (1817-1903),
wife of John Butler, 2nd
Marquess of Ormonde CB

John Butler (1808-1854), 2nd
Marquess of Ormonde CB

Long Gallery,
circa 1890 NLI

THE END OF THE OLD ORDER

The entire world changed rapidly in the first half of the twentieth century. The Irish state changed dramatically, too. During the Civil War, Lord Ossory, son of the Marquess of Ormonde, was caught up in the Irish situation. He later wrote: *It was on the morning of 2nd May 1922 that, at the unreasonable hour of 5.30, I was awakened by a knock at the door. My butler appeared and greeted me with: "Excuse me disturbing your Lordship, but the Republicans have taken the Castle".* They were immediately beseiged by the Free Staters, but the castle was restored to the Butlers after a two-day seige.

The changes in society in Ireland, however, meant that, in the 1930s, the Butlers had to look closely at the viability of maintaining their seat at Kilkenny Castle. In 1935, they decided to leave, and so a great auction was held in the castle. For five days all the contents of the castle were auctioned off; all that remained in the empty castle was the family collection of paintings and tapestries.

Apart from a brief period of occupation by Irish troops during World War II, known as "The Emergency", Kilkenny Castle stood empty and abandoned.

Drawing Room, circa 1890 NLI

BY DIRECTION OF THE RIGHT HON. THE EARL OF OSSORY.

"KILKENNY CASTLE"

Kilkenny, Ireland

MESSIEURS

BATTERSBY & CO.

are favoured with instructions from

THE RIGHT HON. THE EARL OF OSSORY

to Sell by Auction

at

"KILKENNY CASTLE"

THE VALUABLE FURNISHINGS AND
APPOINTMENTS OF THE HISTORIC MANSION

together with the Library, Outdoor Effects, etc.

The Sale will commence on

MONDAY, 18th NOVEMBER, 1935, and 5 following days

and will be resumed on

MONDAY, 25th NOVEMBER, 1935, and 3 following days

At 12 o clock each day.

View Days : Thursday, Friday and Saturday, 14th, 15th and 16th November, from 10 a.m. to 4 p.m. only, owing to short days. This Catalogue admits holder on days of View and Sale.

BATTERSBY & CO.
Auctioneers and Valuers
90 Westmoreland Street, Dublin.
ESTABLISHED 1815.

RESTORATION AGAIN

In 1967, Arthur Butler, sixth Marquess and twenty-fourth Earl of Ormonde, handed Kilkenny Castle over to the Castle Restoration Committee for the nominal sum of £50. In an address he said: *The people of Kilkenny, as well as myself and my family, feel a great pride in the Castle, and we have not liked to see this deterioration. We determined that it should not be allowed to fall into ruins. There are already too many ruins in Ireland.*

Because of the expense involved in restoring such a castle, the building was taken into state care. The early stages of restoration were funded by a generous gift from C.J. Lytle, a London businessman of Irish descent.

After treating the fabric of the entire building for dry rot and wet rot, a phased programme of restoration started. The east wing was re-roofed and completely restored and opened to the public in 1976. As well as the formal reception rooms of the castle, especially the Long Gallery with its restored picture collection, this wing houses the modern Butler Art Gallery in a ground floor suite of former servants' rooms. The old kitchen also operates as a restaurant in the summer season.

The carved Carrara marble fireplace in the Long Gallery

The Kitchen range

The Long Gallery CB

Detail of the Long Gallery roof CB

Left
The Main Hall
and the Ante-room

THE CASTLE PARK

Once the Butlers felt themselves secure here they started to improve the Castle and the surrounding lands for their own comfort and pleasure. Large areas of land were reserved for their sport, for hunting, fishing and shooting, while lands closer to the Castle were developed as private gardens and walks. In the seventeenth century restoration, the Duke had these laid out in the formal style by 'Carrie, your French Gardiner' with 'Bowling green, Gardens, Walks, Orchards and a delightfull Waterhouse adjoining'. These were furnished with elaborate wrought iron gates, with statues and fountains.

In the late eighteenth century Walter Butler moved the approach road away from the Castle, improving the views of the parkland and making it much more private. Many of the mature trees in the Park today date from his improvements, as do the boundary walls.

In the nineteenth century further work to the Park including putting a tennis court, summer houses and an artificial lake at the far end of the Park. This was a reservoir fed by springs, from which water was pumped up to the Castle. The remains of the old pumphouse still stand: this was fuelled by coal brought in from Castlecomer coalmines.

Elaborate plans were drawn up for improving the old terraced garden and the parkland, but due to the death of the Marquess these were not implemented.

No work was done in the Park in the forty years up to its being taken into state care in 1969, nor for some time before that. Initially fifteen acres was handed over to the state. The Castle Park now includes all the walled demesne parkland to the south and the formal terraced garden to the north. The terraced garden has been restored as a rose garden with formal beds of old roses around an impressive fountain. In the parkland an extensive programme of tree planting and maintenance is ongoing. New paths all round the Park have been provided, leading to the children's playground, the small burial ground where the third, fourth, fifth and sixth Marquesses are buried, to the woodland walk and the lake area.

The parklands viewed from the Castle CB

The Castle Park is open every day and is very extensively used both by Kilkenny people and by visitors.

Park scenes GD

*The staff of Kilkenny
Castle and Park*